BE A TRUE YOGI

Do You Have What It Takes?

A comprehensive guide to building a solid foundation for your spiritual journey

ADIGURU PRAKRITI

ISBN: 9798887839196

PREFACE

The subject of this book, wisdom, is derived from my own spiritual journey and should not be taken as the only way to be. There can be paths as numerous as there are people, and there can be innumerable ways to experience and explain all this. None of my advice should be treated as a substitute for medicine, medical treatments, any type of counselling, etc. The spiritual journey is about seeing yourself in the mirror, naked! It requires a great deal of courage to walk this path. Many Hindi/Sanskrit terms are used in this book due to the unavailability of English equivalent translations, though approximate translated terms/words are also provided for easier understanding.

We acknowledge all Aboriginal and Torres Strait Islander Traditional Custodians of Country (Australia) and recognise their continuing connection to land, sea, culture, and community. We pay our respects to Elders, past and present. Aboriginal, Indigenous and Torres Strait Islander people of Australia are advised that this book may contain the description and details of the dead people and sacred places. Reader discretion is advised.

You will have to read this book with an open mind and heart as many concepts may be new to you and may not fit into your preconceived belief system. Indeed, the information in this book may shatter your social conditioning.

I am a Candle, Burning Bright, and you are a candle in need of light. I can give you light; but for that, you must burn! No Exceptions!

No book or content publishing can ever happen without a few people burning the midnight oil. Special thanks to Parveen and Aparna and heartfelt gratitude for volunteering to bring this book to reality and helping me share the wisdom.

Adiguru Prakriti

ABOUT THE AUTHOR

Adiguru Prakriti is an Enlightened, Self-Realised Kriya and Tantra Guru who is a reincarnated disciple of Great Kriya Yoga Guru Shri Lahiri Mahasaya. In this life, her Kundalini was Awakened in 2011, and through opened Guru Chakra and visions of Guru Lahiri Mahasaya, she walked her journey and did her remaining Sadhana until she was Enlightened on 5th March 2015. Months-long Samadhi led her towards Self-Realisation in 2016. She was born and raised in India, lived in the USA for more than a decade and now is living in Melbourne, Australia. After completing her own journey, she started teaching people around the world through the organisation she founded, "Being Shiva Foundation".

Adiguru Prakriti

Founder, Chairperson

Being Shiva Foundation

Web www.BeingShiva.org www.YogiParampara.org

Email BeingShivaFoundation@yahoo.com

Address Melbourne, Victoria, Australia

ABOUT THE BEING SHIVA FOUNDATION

Being Shiva Foundation is a charitable, non-profit organisation founded by Adiguru Prakriti and dedicated to cultivating and nurturing the ultimate human possibilities. The foundation is a human service organisation that helps people attain spiritual liberation by helping them walk their spiritual journey. It is a movement towards a Global Consciousness Breakthrough via individual transformation.

The foundation is operated by a team of volunteers and is headquartered in the beautiful and most livable city of Melbourne, Australia. The organisation provides courses, programs, techniques, retreats and talks through various channels to empower people for spiritual healing, shedding the false self, cultivating yogic/spiritual lifestyle, striving for physical, mental, emotional, and energetic well-being.

When human beings experience trauma or severe life stressors, it is not uncommon for their lives to unravel; the emotional wound is pushed deep inside, and they are forced to find answers to questions like "why me?" To answer this painful call from modern-age men, women, youth, teens, Adiguru Prakriti has developed Inner Transformation programs, Meditation and Spiritual Healing techniques based on ancient yogic science, which are now being used by many people worldwide.

Being Shiva Foundation, a vibrant spiritual community, is also dedicated to several other human service projects with the goals of supporting individual growth in distressed times, rebuilding human relationships and energising the environment positively by changing individual energy signatures, the Aura. Modern science has proven that it purifies the collective consciousness, reduces crime, and helps elevate humanity by raising the energy vibrations higher up to the vibrational frequency for love and compassion. Group meditation and Satsang sessions by the Foundation are a movement towards achieving global peacefulness through alleviating the pain and suffering of human life.

Chapters

WHO IS NOT A YOGI?

People feel very happy when they get a spiritual name, and if Yogi is added to their spiritual name, then their excitement reaches cloud nine. They take on a new identity while the entire yogic path and the meditation and spiritual journey are all about removing all your identities. So, the first thing that you must keep in mind is when you get a spiritual name, do not create an identity.

The main reason it has been given to you is so that whatever your former name was, you can start detaching from it. It will also provide you with a name that connotes deep spiritual meaning rather than either being meaningless or that of some historical figure who may or may not be seen in a good light through the lens of spirituality. Regardless, you shouldn't adopt it as a new identity as you are about to embark on the journey of leaving all fake identities and their web behind. Receiving the spiritual name as part of initiation doesn't make one a Yogi.

Mostly, all those who are embarking on their spiritual practices religiously and seriously are yogis in process. They may or may not be true yogis yet, even though they may be living in an ashram or monastery. Cladding themselves in yogic adornments like mala, beads, charms, pendants, etc., doesn't guarantee their yogi-ness either. Don't judge the book by its cover.

Anyone who has attachments to material or spiritual identities, worlds, theories, philosophies, practices, rituals or who has an aversion to infinite things, people, and situations or is fearful like a bird or a fish is not a yogi. The one who resists the changes in life and will not stand for truth both within and without is not a yogi. Then, who is a yogi?

WHO IS A YOGI?

A Yogi is the one who lives by heart, by open and balanced Anahata chakra (Heart Chakra). A Yogi is fearless, possessing a pure intellect, wearing his/her heart on their sleeve and taking a stand for himself/herself and others for anything just and truthful. From the perspective of Maharishi Patanjali's Yoga Sutras, a Yogi is devoid of attachments (Raga), aversions (Dwesha), fears and resistance to change (Abhinivesha) and is an intense being. A yogi is a conscious being to a greater extent. When you walk your spiritual journey, there will be times when you will be fearful because your astral body starts coming alive. You will start having different kinds of experiences, handling and dealing with the karmas of your different lifetimes, including this lifetime. You must face all that you have ever done, good and bad. There will be fearful times, but a yogi is the one who does not stop despite fears, limitations, boundaries, and social conditioning. Nothing stops a yogi from walking the spiritual journey. That is who a yogi is. The one who lives from the heart, from the open and balanced Anahata chakra, is not living for this world, this society. He/she is not playing the games of expectations and obligations in the name of relationships in life. A yogi doesn't procrastinate. Certainly, a yogi is not a people pleaser at all . . . quite the opposite. A yogi is not a being who goes by the social and moral codes. A yogi lives for Truth, for righteousness. Yogis do not fabricate a web of fakery around themselves. In other words, they do not abide by social or mental constructs or the social conditioning that has been given to people since childhood. They are never one of the sheep in the flock. They stand alone and, most of the time, they walk alone. The spiritual journey is walked alone; it's a very deep, serious, private matter between a Yogi and the Divine.

A Yogi's life is not about following an individual or a current trend; it's always about being truthful, being who they are at any given point of time and not trying to abide by crowd truth. Yogis can see the futility of living life while wearing the rosy glasses of Maya (Illusions). Yogis understand the root cause of suffering, which is not relationships, heartbreaks, or materially unsuccessful life, but spiritual ignorance – in other words, not knowing the existential Truth. Living from the open and balanced Anahata helps a Yogi look at themselves without illusions, which is the hardest thing to do. Being Yogi is about facing yourself, facing your deep, hardened psychological patterns (Chitta Vrittis) and then having the determination to work on them, to fix and transform oneself. The goal of human life is to transform oneself to achieve the ultimate potential of being a human and add divinity to it. Being a Yogi is the start. Know that until the Anahata chakra is opened and balanced, you have not started on your real spiritual journey.

SANCTITY IN LIFE

Attaining sanctity is one of the most important preparations you must make before you start your spiritual path or practice. You need to achieve that sanctity. Sanctity is not just for the physical body. You will see a lot of people being fanatical about physical sanctity, cultivating aversions to types of food, modes of sleeping, bathing habits, etc. It's not bad to be mindful of all that while walking your spiritual journey. But creating new attachments, likes and aversions, dislikes and reacting out of fears and resisting any change could be the reversal of all your spiritual practices.

You do have to maintain some physical sanctity, like taking a shower and cleansing your physical body, but don't be obsessive about it. If there is a problem in your body, then take precautions, take prescribed medications and maintain it well, like the way in which you would maintain your nice car or house. No need to go to extreme lengths and make the 5% of your existence a bigger deal, ignoring 95% and creating new psychological patterns (Chitta

Vrittis). Know that sanctifying your subtle existence is much more beneficial for your spiritual journey. Being physically pure yet mentally dirty is not going to work in your favour.

Nature maintains sanctity too. All kinds of trees, birds, flowers and water in a pond and the mountains also maintain sanctity and purity. That is the reason when you go into nature, you suddenly find yourself very peaceful and joyful; those who can connect with nature know what I am talking about. How do you feel when you are out in a forest?

During my childhood in India, I played in the backyard, in the forest reserve behind our house. I used to climb trees, catch snakes, and handle a lot of wildlife. It was a magical time for me, a mystical time for me. And I learned how things are in so much harmony all the time in nature. When roots are inside the ground, they might be looking for water or life or oxygen or nitrogen or all those things, but from the top, you can see that one tree is supporting the other, and each one is taking resources only as per their need. One tree is leaning on the other tree, and it's perfectly fine. In nature, everything is interconnected. There is no fake world or separate identities of different plants and trees spreading lies and competing for resources. There is authenticity and integrity in nature. Know that that is what sanctifies it, purifies it.

Similarly, when you walk your spiritual path, you must sanctify yourself and be authentic and be integrated and pure-hearted . . . not just from the point of view of your physical body (Annamaya Kosha) but in your thoughts and emotions (Manomaya Kosha) as well.

If your head is full of negative thoughts and emotions that

undermine you or someone else, if you feel you are always in a race, in a competition with someone for something, or you feel guilty for being this way or that way or play the blame game, then that means your psychological world, your inner world is polluted. If you try to be a people pleaser most of the time and you feel one way yet think another or say something different from what you are thinking, and your actions match neither your thoughts nor your speech, then you are deeply polluted, to the core, all the way to the root chakra (Muladhara Chakra).

This means you are not maintaining the sanctity. However cleaned or groomed your physical body might be, however many white shirts or white pants you may wear, you do not have sanctity in your inner world. If you love to speak or accept lies or half-truths because the truth is too hard to bear, then that means you neither love yourself nor do you love other people. You have not made a heartfelt surrender (Samarpan) to the life that is around you.

This is enough to realize that your Heart Chakra (Anahata Chakra) is closed. You are always fearful about what wrong may happen or what other people may do to you or how much of a chance there is that you will be betrayed and what needs to be done if you are betrayed and how to handle life by living and reacting through fears.

If you are always fearful and instead of choosing to love, you choose to fear, and your fears give rise to anger and rage and you find yourself being cruel to others, then know that the pollution is at an all-time high and has completely blocked the root chakra (Muladhara).

Sanctity in your inner world, your thoughts and emotions is of utmost importance. You can live consciously, do Pranayama

(Breathing Exercises), and practice Hatha Yoga to remove all the impurities from within.

Next is the sanctity, purity of energy and your etheric body (Pranamaya Kosha). How do we attain and maintain that?

There are all kinds of negative people around you. The world is full of them. You try doing one thing, and people will come and tell you no, you shouldn't be doing that.

They will project their own fears and insecurities no matter what you do. Even if you try to get out of a bad relationship, you will find people who will convince you not to, convince you that you shouldn't get out; after all, what if you will not be able to live or survive alone, emotionally and financially? This is the way negative people or negativity surrounds you.

When you go into nature, there is no negativity. Nature is not doubting you, not trying to trip you. Nature is not happening as a reaction to fear. Nature is peaceful, and there is harmony. It is not purposefully throwing bad carbon dioxide on you as other people go on throwing negative thoughts and negative energy on you. So, you need to be careful about that. You need to stay away from those who don't understand your path, who do not understand what you are doing and why. There comes a time when you should learn to firmly say no to people, their ideas, and their projections on you.

When I was walking my spiritual path, there came a time when I went into a sort of seclusion from people, from society, from everyone around me as no one would know this new me and her struggles. No one could comprehend my inner world, my state. For them, I was just another round peg in a square hole. Yet, for some, I was just another worldly, social creature going around living life, leading the corporate world in information technology. No one knew that I was getting up at 2:30-3 a.m., starting my spiritual practices from 3:40 a.m. sharp. The people, the society around me, didn't know that I was awake all night, two or three times a week, just writing and reading. Thousands of ideas sparked into my mind, and I was busy in a very different world. No one could understand or see that I was transforming every day. No one was aware that I was doing contemplative meditation all the time, even as I was surrounded by people and seemingly busy with mundane work. Deep down, I was trying to catch my remaining psychological patterns (Chitta-Vrittis & Sanskaras) and was hell-bent on removing my spiritual ignorance and existential ignorance (Agyan/Avidya). And when you are deeply, seriously busy with your inner world, you don't want to get into small talk with people just for the sake of it. You don't want to do useless talking. Better to get rid of them; let them think and believe whatever they want about you. Your life, your transformation, and your recognition don't come from such people but from the great Almighty Divine. Be busy becoming a better version of yourself, hour by hour, day by day.

I was a reserved individual, an introvert who never liked small talks for the sake of formality or out of obligation. Unless there was a dire necessity to say something, I wouldn't say a word. Neither did I want to prove myself, nor did I have any need to undermine the person who was in front of me. Neither was there a need to show my inner reality to anyone nor was it anyone's business. A lot is left unanswered, and that's way much better than what you could ever say. In any case, people hear and understand according to their filters. Those who truly love you understand you do not depend on your verbality and those who do not love or understand you . . . for them, your words do not mean anything anyway.

Know that not everyone is ready to handle the bigger truth. You may be on your journey of awakening; others around you still want to enjoy their sleep and dreams. So be it; let them. Do not disturb.

When you are walking your spiritual path, you need to stay away from many people; rarely would anyone understand your journey. Don't think that just because we all are humans, we all have developed the human body, that everyone is at the same level. That's one big mistake. You may think that just because someone is older than you or maybe of your age, your profession, your culture and speaks your language and is in love with you, they will understand what you are going through and might be able to help you, support you. It's quite the opposite. Your only reliance is on your Guru or yourself (inner Guru).

Everyone is a different bundle of Karma and psychological patterns (Chitta Vrittis), despite having the same age, gender, and culture. A being comes into existence as human many times, and not everyone has been here that many times and may not have made the kind of good choices to be wise enough to be able to help you, support you or guide you. Just because you have started on your path of being a true Yogi, not everyone can become that, despite their desire to be one. It requires a serious commitment to oneself, towards one's own transformation. That commitment will take your breath away, will turn your life upside down, and will make it painful to see the illusionary, impermanent nature of all that is.

A very few people are born with an open and balanced Heart Chakra (Anahata Chakra). They follow the path of truth and righteousness. It requires a lot of courage. They choose truth over fear, choose truth over cheating, lying and all those things. In this day and age, such courageous, openhearted people are rare, and I can't say you must surround yourself only with people like them. But at least you know now with what kind of people you should not surround yourself. And that is very important in maintaining the sanctity of your life. Know that when I talk about people, I am also referring to those 'online' ones who may show their face to you only once in a blue moon yet may live in your body-mind all the time.

Now, these days, another kind of sanctity is needed, which is through the limited use of your mobile phone, tablets, laptops, and digital devices. While I was walking my spiritual journey for two and a half years, I was not on any social media at all. I rarely looked at my phone; only when somebody called would I pick it up. And that too because I stayed away from all the social circle and friends and people around me; nobody was calling me anyway. But I still used to have a phone for emergencies, contingencies from my son's school or somebody or something from the job needs my immediate attention and help, and I needed to get involved. So, for those reasons, I had a phone. Otherwise, I did not indulge in any social media or videos.

In the early mornings, I did some kriya yoga and then shortly landed into lower levels of Samadhis (Savikalpa, Sabeeja). Throughout the day, working in corporate and being a single mother, I was doing contemplative meditation. I walked my spiritual journey through inner Guru, inner guidance, Ritambhara Pragya (Highest, purest state of Intellect) and with an understanding that Samadhi or Meditation is a natural state of a human being, then what is it in me that disturbed it, destroyed it? So, I did a great deal of introspection, focusing on what disturbed my state of Samadhi and realized that those are the seeds of the psychological patterns (Sanskaras and Chitta Vrittis) and my existential spiritual ignorance. It is because of spiritual ignorance

(Agyan/Avidya) that we create those psychological patterns (Sanskaras and Chitta Vrittis) in the first place. We do not have the correct wisdom: otherwise, why would we sow the seeds of weeds? We do not have the right perception of life, truth, or existence.

Then I used to ask, alright, what's the right perception? Now, because in 2011, when my Kundalini awakened and as a result, Guru Chakra was opened, Ritambhara Pragya was achieved, hence within a day or two, I would get an answer to all the questions that I asked my inner Guru. That's how I kept going and transforming myself with good speed.

You may not yet have your inner Guru awakened and may not have attained Ritambhara Pragya, so you can take help from the outer Gurus, human Gurus. So, those were the times when I strictly maintained sanctity, not just physical, even refraining from shaking hands at the office or hugging people, but sanctity at all levels of my existence.

The care you must take to maintain purity and sanctity is not permanent; once your journey reaches the advanced levels and sanctity is sustained through your inner fires, you will not need to do anything externally. The universe will take care of everything for you and will give you immense strength and energy such that nothing from outside can do anything to you. The day will come when you will not be impacted by anything, anyone at all. The day will come when all that is will not exist for you.

When a child starts walking, we try to protect him from all the sharp edges, and we try to remove obstacles from his path. And when he gains the strength and balance to start walking and running by himself, we don't need to do all those things. Similarly, you need to maintain sanctity for the time while you are walking your spiritual journey. Once you are successful, however long it may take, then you can come back into the world, and nothing could disturb or pollute anything in your existence because it's ultimately a very beautiful world, a very beautiful creation of the Creator.

Sanctity must also be achieved prior to traveling to any guru's ashram or monastery to attend a course, a program or a retreat or to receive Initiation (Deeksha). It takes some time to cultivate enough sanctity to be able to get the best out of the program, retreat, initiation or your meeting with the Guru. You are not going to have it overnight. Don't be childish; don't attempt to fool yourself.

Cultivating sanctity is a preparatory thing. Don't try to do preparatory stuff afterwards or while you are with the guru, or when you are in the retreat or program. No. That's a wrong thing. You are wasting your retreat, program, your energy, and money. You are wasting your time while you are with the Guru. And above all, you are wasting the time of an Enlightened one.

Know that on any given day, in this era (Yuga), hardly 200 Enlightened ones are alive, and only a few of them are available to stand as Guru for the world and its people. Do not waste their time. You need to do preparatory stuff before you go to your guru or before you start your spiritual practices or sadhana or before you go to any retreat, or before you start attending the program with your spiritual Guru. When you build a solid foundation of sanctity, you will be able to take full advantage of what the Guru is offering to you, what you are being taught, and what initiations will propel you in the right direction.

Sanctity, purity, authenticity, and integrity in life demand a complete change in your inner world and outer life. And it is a must not only for your spiritual upliftment but also for your healing at the physical and psychological levels. Without it, no doctor, psychologist, psychiatrist, or healer can ever heal you or even treat you. And if, somehow, by the grace of the divine and force of nature, they can, then your disease, your problem will come back again; it's only a matter of time. Hence, it's important for your overall well-being as well.

The sanctity of the intellect is explained in the diagram below.

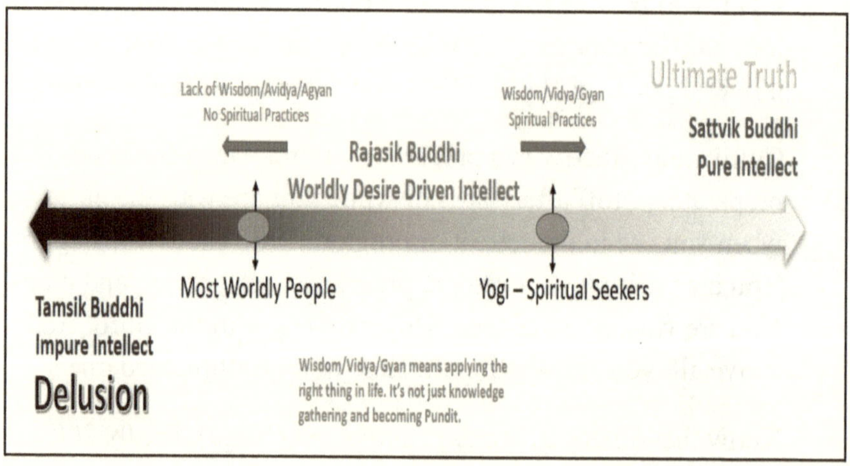

PHYSICAL and MENTAL DETOX

Before you join any kind of spiritual practice, yoga or meditation camp, you need to detoxify your body. How do you detoxify your body? First, you need to adjust your routine for eating. The fire that cooks the food in your stomach, which digests the food, is called Jatharagni. That Jatharagni is very strong around the hours of sunrise and around the hours of sunset. You should try to arrange and align your mealtimes around those times. After your last meal, there should be a gap of four hours before you go to sleep. Otherwise, if you have food in your stomach, your mind is definitely going to fire thousands of crazy thoughts. You cannot sleep properly. There will be gastric trouble in your stomach, and you will be restless all night long. Even during the day, if you have food stuck in your intestines, then it's a very disturbing time and your thoughts per second will increase if your stomach and your intestines are not clean.

Now, what is the way to clean them? As mentioned, the first thing to do is fix your eating routine. Another thing to pay attention to is that along with food, you need to start eating something that detoxifies your blood and your body such as aloe vera juice. Or you can try the triphala herb, another ayurvedic herbal mix of three herbs – amla, harad and baheda. Or you can start taking haritaki, another herb that detoxifies your system. So, you can take anything that detoxifies and is available in your country or city. Some people drink juice; others prefer fasting. Beware, if you are on any medications, you first need to consult with your doctor before taking any herbs or before fasting or juicing to make sure you are not making any mistakes, and you're not making a wrong chemical composition for your body. Don't just read something on the Internet; you can go to a good Ayurvedic doctor for consultation as well.

If possible, you also need to start taking ghee (Indian cow ghee) if it is possible. If Indian desi ghee is available to you, then you should start eating that, a couple of teaspoonfuls every day. Why I am saying that is because every food item that you eat has three elements – gross, medium, and subtle. When digested, the gross element becomes stool and is excreted. For example, if you eat bread or anything made up of wheat or rice, the fibre becomes excretory material. In all the food items that you are eating, there is little absorption material for the subtle body; most becomes stool. Rarely does any food item become some part of your subtle body, your subtle existence. Ghee is one food that does not have any gross parts in it. That means desi ghee doesn't go out of your body. The medium part of Ghee creates bones and bone marrow and the subtle part of Ghee nourishes the mind (Manas). It nourishes your psychological body (Manomaya Kosha). So, this is how it works. Now, here I am, not talking about clarified butter. I lived in

America, and now I'm living here in Australia. Many people will just go and buy the cream, and then they will heat it up and after it is cooked enough, they will just strain sell it at the store, calling it ghee. No, that is not ghee. Butter is from cream; ghee is comprised of yogurt or dahi and, unlike cream or butter, contains an active culture. You can keep clarified butter or butter oil for a very long time. You cannot do that with ghee; it has a short shelf life and must be consumed within a certain amount of time; it has a short shelf life. But there's a limit to eating anything. You cannot just drink Ghee and lots of Ghee. No, don't do that. Consume Ghee in a limited amount. Be moderate in consumption of even the good things.

Another thing that you need to consider is drinking water. A lot of you are so habitual of drinking green tea, drinking vitamin water or drinking energy drinks in the name of quenching your thirst. You go on taking so many other things but water. Do not do that. That's a grave mistake you are making. Your body runs on Prana Shakti (Vital Life Force). Prana in you is only created, nourished through water. Whenever you are consuming pure water, just plain simple pure water, then your body is nourishing, creating prana out of it. Suppose you start consuming green tea when you are thirsty or energy drinks or cold drinks or some soda or anything like that . . . your body will not be able to immediately convert that into prana right away. So, whenever your body is signalling you or whenever you are feeling thirsty, then it's not only a signal that your physical body needs water or that it is dehydrated but also a signal that your Etheric Body (Pranamaya Kosha) needs more Vital Life Force (Pranic Shakti). Hence, you should be drinking plain, simple water.

While you are actively involved in your physical detoxification, you must start a mental detoxification routine as well. Now, what is mental detoxification? You all have people around you who are happy gossiping. Some people are addicted to their worries, fears, insecurities, and opinions. There could be infinite varieties of addictions in people's minds, and they may just come to you and vomit them all over you . . . their thoughts, all their nonsense and whatnot. You need to start staying away from such people because then it goes on and on. The judge in your head goes on very busy active duty. What everybody tells you or what these kinds of people tell you just goes on and on in your head, and you also go on endlessly judging them. As a result, you create more toxins than you release. So, if you have a detoxification routine, say, for example, 40 days, and you are trying to carefully cleanse your physical body but, every day, there are people who will just puke on you, push your buttons and get on your nerves, your physical detoxification will fail as well.

Compulsive talkers and chatterboxes are of no use to anyone. They will drain your Pranic Shakti (Vital Life Force). You need to stay away from such people so that your mind is less polluted and not over-functional. Your physical body is the secondary thing. The first and foremost thing is your mind, your mental-emotional body. If you can maintain or detoxify your mind, then it's easy to detoxify your body. But if you are just detoxifying your body and not your mind, then that is like trying to put money in a pocket that has a hole in it or trying to fill a broken bucket with water.

It's of no use. Instead of a purification routine taking 40 days, it may take months for you to baseline yourself.

The first detoxification that you need to do is of your mind and your thoughts. Try becoming calm. Stop being too reactive as well, and, for some time, stay away from people who provoke you. This is not a permanent situation; someday you will be capable of controlling your reactions. This is like when a child is learning to stand or walk, a mother will hold their hand, but that's a temporary situation. Some day that child will start walking or running by himself and won't need anyone to hold his hand. In the same way, right now, this mental and emotional or physical detoxification is needed, and we are taking certain measures to do it. But once you learn to stand up for yourself, you do not need to push people out of your life. If you want to, you can, but you don't have to do it for this reason.

Hence, remember to drink plain water and take something that detoxifies your body and stay away from those who disturb your peace or are full of negative energy or whichever way you want to look at that. I understand that a lot of you will say that your living conditions make this difficult. If that is the situation, then I would say at least for some time, if you can go away or you can send them away or if even that is not possible, then try to control your reactions for some time because frequently bursting into anger is not going to detoxify your system. It won't help. And anger doesn't do anything; holding grudges or feeling guilty or feeling all kinds of low and negative emotions is not going to help you in any way. Hence while you are on your detoxifying routine, be less reactive. Follow these detoxification routines before joining any kind of yoga, meditation program, retreat or receiving initiation from any Guru. Detoxification makes you lighter, a little emptier, and elevates your entire existence by helping you expand your consciousness. When you attain a good level of detoxed mind and body, only then will Shakti and initiations work for you because, only then, will you be receptive to wisdom from the Guru.

A detoxed mind and body are also important for your overall well-being, your focus, and your attention span and will help you succeed in any area of your life.

BEING IN NATURE

Why is it so important to be in nature? When you are walking your spiritual journey, it is about keeping your etheric body, your energy body pure, so it can expand effortlessly. And the easiest way to do it is by being in nature. Forests, waterfalls, gorges, huge trees, the whole ecosystem of a jungle electrifies and purifies your etheric body quickly. You can walk or stand barefoot for a few minutes in the natural waterfalls or on the soil/earth of the forest, and it can supercharge you by taking the negative ions away from your body and restoring the balance. Deep breathing in nature can intensify your consciousness and your Pranic Shakti (Vital Life Force).

You are made up of the same five elements – earth, water, fire, air and space/ether – that nature contains. These five elements, which create your existence, create all that is; the entire creation is made up of different combinations of one or more of these elements. That is what you have all around you in abundance, hence the reason your physical body, your subtle bodies, and your existence find affinity with nature easily, and nature, in turn, helps purify your existence. Doing hard spiritual practices (Tapasya) in the Himalayas is not just a fanciful idea. When a gathering of people do Tapasya or a spiritual sadhana at one place, the energy signature of that place changes.

I have been sensitive to places since I was born; I could see and perceive through my subtle existence the past events of places. And I have been to many forests, and natural places in America and here in Australia and have done overnight camping deep in the forests, only to realize painfully that those were the places where hundreds and thousands of Native Americans and Aboriginal Indigenous people were raped, killed and butchered mercilessly, and I can feel the pain and darkness in the etheric energy all around.

Yes, trees, waterfalls, and gorges may look beautiful at first sight, but the energy doesn't feel right. If you stay there for some time, you start getting knots in and around your naval and throat area. Staying there overnight is not easy and may overwhelm your etheric body for weeks, if not months.

Before I came to Melbourne, Australia, I mystically encountered and contacted an old man named John, an architect by profession from Melbourne, who discussed ley lines and powerful energy vortexes in Australia. He told me how he and some of his friends had spent almost thirty years uplifting the hundreds and thousands of dead souls of aboriginal people of this land, this place of Melbourne and Victoria, through a Dreamtime Portal and how he and his group has helped them cross over, instead of staying stuck here. He wrote the book, *Portal to the Dreamtime*.

After I landed here in Melbourne, I went to see him, and we talked for a long time. He said it was clear to him now that he was cleaning the etheric plane of Melbourne and Victoria so that an Enlighted Being like me could come and live here and make this place her home. He smiled and said *I was cleaning it for you; yes, that was the purpose . . . now I know*. There was truth in it. Earlier,

I had plans to live and settle in Sydney, but somehow last minute, mystically, I was guided to land in Melbourne instead, and on my very first evening here in Melbourne, I had a deep realization that I was home, this was the city, the place where I was going to live. Then mystical beings just led me to a house which is quite close to the energy vortex, which John named *Oasis Anu Ta,* where he did his works of helping souls' crossover for almost 30 years. Later, he wrote another book, *Lifting the Veils,* where he mentioned this knowing and my meeting with him and his realization of the purpose of doing the cleansing of the etheric plane. When he was young, in his twenties, he has been to India, and he gave me a copy of his photo with Pandit Jawahar Lal Nehru, the then Prime Minister of India.

The point to understand here is that just like you carry the memory (we call it Karma) of your ancestors, the history of past generations in your physical body, in your psychological body, similarly, the forests and other places can retain the memories of good and bad events too. After all, forests are made up of the same five elements that constitute our gross existence.

Quite the opposite is the Himalayas. If you ever visit India and you visit the Himalayas, Ganges, Bhagirathi River, Gangotri Glacier region and any other small village or town in the Himalayan region, then you will know what I am talking about. Every kilometre of the land, there has a temple of Shakti or Shiva, or village deity (Gram Devata), and active worship goes on there in the morning and evening. You can hear the mantra chanting early morning and evening, yet sometimes for hours during the day as well on special occasions like the nine days of Shakti/Goddess (Navratri). You can smell fragrant herbs and incense sticks most of the time. You can see Sadhu/Sanyasi (Spiritual Renunciates), Yogis absorbed in meditation and yoga sadhana (spiritual practices). There are Gurus and Ashrams (Monasteries) all around.

Mantras echo in the Himalayas even when no one is chanting. Sound is energy that is never lost; that's how scientists were able to retrieve and record the sounds from world wars and other past events. Since the time immemorial, the Himalayas have been the place chosen by the great Gurus and Enlightened Beings to pursue their spiritual journeys. That whole place has a powerfully uplifting spiritual energy. If your subtle bodies (Koshas) are pure enough, you will be overwhelmed by the love, peace, and bliss (Sat-Chit-Ananda) of that area. There, your entire existence may start vibrating at a higher frequency, and its effect will not wear out easily. Naturally, your consciousness is expanded when you are in the Himalayas, and it is easier to quickly transform yourself. Your spiritual practices fructify easily there.

Hence, many spiritual folks just want to run to India and stay in the Himalayas. Some are serious about their spiritual journey, while some are soaking in the experience, the high vibrational energy. Nonetheless, it benefits if one can keep his or her activities there to a minimum and calm themselves, sanctify themselves before hopping on the plane.

Where there are no Himalayas, you will still find a lot of beautiful mountains and rivers flowing, and you can go to such places often and stay some time in nature.

In earlier times, the spiritual people or the Yogis used to do their spiritual practices (Tapasya) where their energy was not going to be compromised. Doing spiritual practices while living in high-rise cities is a bit difficult job as it is difficult to retain the positive, elevated energy. The floors are carpeted, or if they are not carpeted, they have vinyl or cement. Even if you have wooden floors, there is an artificial plastic lining underneath to prevent moisture. So, you're not walking on the earth. If you were, the earth would simply take away the negative ions that you have.

Because of your reactionary living, emotional upheavals, and your limited way of understanding life, the existential truths, you mostly have dense, dark, negative energy lingering in your etheric body. If you look at your Aura through the Kirlian camera and photographic methods, you can see how bad it looks. Science has proven that negative energy, or the dark, dense energy which is lingering in your etheric body, can be easily released when you walk barefoot on the earth or spend some time in nature. It naturally happens; it's effortless. Hence the reason you feel lighter. And doing your spiritual practices in nature gives much better results.

It's easier to be meditative in peaceful surroundings and forests. There's tremendous health benefit as well. Many people are sick today because of all kinds of chemicals in the air and electromagnetic, infrared radiations and vibrations that the body receives from electronic and digital devices. And there is no way that they can even get a proper diagnosis for their health problems . . . forget about getting treatment and a cure.

Therefore, it is highly recommended for you, if you are living a city life and you have a forest area around or whatever mountains area nearby, just go there.

Throughout my spiritual journey, I was in the wilderness as much as possible, and I used to go to many forests, waterfalls, freshwater springs, and natural reserves in America. Even after the completion of my journey, I can't stop myself from being in nature and being one with nature.

You must connect with nature and be one with everything there is. If it is safe for you, then you can try to do your sadhana (Spiritual Practices) in the mountains or near flowing rivers or waterfalls. It's much more fruitful. It works. Know that it is easier to be one with nature than with people. Learn and feel oneness with nature first, then oneness with people will follow, and you will be able to pave the way for oneness with all that is.

Your Heart Chakra (Anahata Chakra) will be balanced if you spend more time in nature. Even today, hundreds and thousands of Yogis choose to live in deep hidden caves in the Himalayas to pursue their spiritual journey, and they live there for decades.

EMOTIONAL RELEASE

Before you embark on your spiritual journey, emotional release is necessary. Just like you detoxify your body, you need to do the detoxification of your emotions as well. You may have restrained yourself from laughing fully, from enjoying life, from crying when you needed because of the silly advice from others around you, or you may have understood emotional expression as a sign of weakness. Society and those around you might have stopped you from expressing your grief or your joy.

Well, if you laugh too much, you will cry afterwards. So that's when you control your laughter, your joy in your heart. And that's when you suppress the grief within.

Regardless of whose doing it is, you have suffocated emotions, creating an abyss of pain and suffering within. It's not good. You do not want to be in emotional turmoil while your Guru, Master, is giving you Existential Wisdom or Spiritual Initiation (Deeksha).

You will not be able to have a one-pointed focus (Dharana) and will not be able to meditate (Dhyana) unless you first have an emotional release.

Many spiritual practices of Kriya Yoga are geared toward helping with emotional release and relief. When you go through life, your understanding of situations, events and people depends upon how awakened you are, how many blocked chakras you have or, in other words, what psychological patterns (Sanskaras and Chitta Vrittis) you were born with, how many you are still carrying and if you have the required existential wisdom.

A lot is poured into you through parents, teachers, mentors, friends, and guides, which we refer to as social conditioning. You may be grieving silently and introspecting yourself, yet your family and friends will try to tell you that you need to busy yourself with mundane work or activities that can help you 'ignore' the sadness, the pain. You listen to them and, temporarily, you feel alright.

Years later when you start your spiritual practices, all that you 'ignored' or suppressed emotion starts to come out, and you wonder what suddenly happened. Grief is just one example. Likewise, you may have suppressed anger, powerlessness or ignorance itself.

For a time, you felt happier living with such ignorance, until you started your spiritual journey. This is one reason why initially, many people become much more sad and go through tough emotional turbulences upon finding or meeting an Enlightened being or spiritual Guru, a Master.

You need to release all your pent-up emotions or emotional energy. If you need to know what kriya yoga practices can be done, you can reach out to us or go through the 'Kriya Yoga' online course. Here is the link for that –
https://www.iidharma.com/courses/AncientPrinciplesOfKriyaYoga

To speed up the process of emotional release, you need to do a little introspection by going through the laundry list of all the bad situations and unfavourable circumstances that life has put you through, the heartbreaks that you've had, and the humiliation and emotional let-downs that you faced. Make a list of all bad events and the emotions connected to them that you suppressed.

Sit down with yourself and peek into your memory. This exercise will help you accept what you have within. You may feel it as a heaviness in your chest because of suppressed grief, burning within if it was anger or a choked kind of feeling around the throat area if your voice, your expression was suppressed.

Releasing all this stuff will make you lighter, will help you focus and concentrate and do Dharana/one-pointedness and will later lead you to dhyana/meditation. Think about it seriously.

Many of you are trying to achieve perfection in your One-Pointed focus (Dharana) and trying to meditate (Dhyana), and it's not working because you have pent-up emotions; you have suffocated yourself, and you have suppressed emotional energy to weigh you down.

Until that negative energy is released from your existence, you will not find calm within and will not achieve stability in your body and mind. Hence, consider it seriously, have an acceptance within and then work on the methods and techniques that can help you release that energy.

Emotional release is not only required for your spiritual growth but also helps you to have a disease-free healthy body. These suffocated emotions later will manifest in your physical body. Pent-up emotions like fear and anger will manifest as diseases or health issues related to the kidneys.

Feeling unloved or unworthy will manifest as heart problems and so on. Different types of choked emotions manifest as health issues in different organs. Now, who would want a sick body? You cannot pursue your spiritual practices with a sick body.

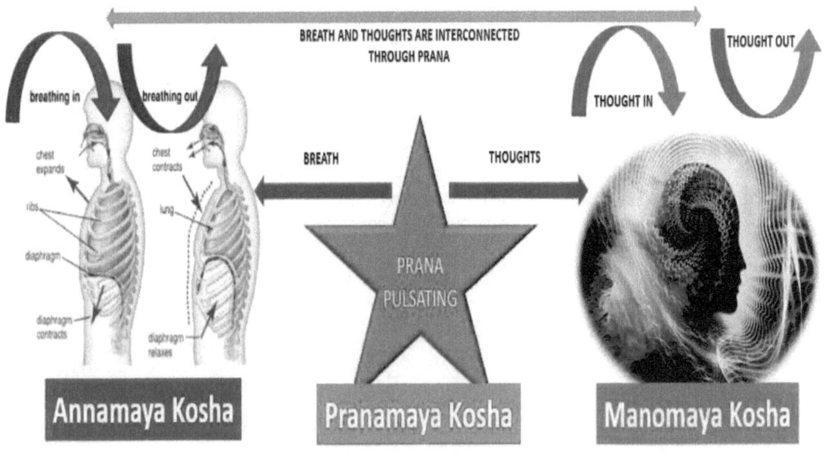

PROPER BREATHING

Why is breathing so important for learning any kind of yoga, even before you join a yoga or any tantra, mantra, Yantra, or any kind of spiritual practice or meditation camp? Before joining that kind of program, you first need to understand breathing. And not only understand it for 30 days before you go to that program, but you also need to practice the proper way of breathing. If you do not understand and practice the proper way of breathing, then there is no point; whatever you are trying to do is not going to work for you – the yoga, the Pranayama, all these things do not work. Pranayama comes after you understand and practice the proper way of breathing, and your breathing is regularised and normalized; only then can you be taught Pranayama.

So, what type of breathing are we talking about? Most of you, those who are working in offices and have stress, anxiety, this that, 30-plus people, 40-plus people I have seen, they have forgotten how to breathe properly. They are constantly breathing from the chest. Now, if you keep on breathing shallowly from the chest, it activates the fight-or-flight system in your body. And when that system is activated, your body, your entire existence, your body energy, everything is in the mode of either fight or flight.

Now, imagine you are working on your laptop or your computer or on your office desk, you are sitting and doing mental work, but your body is in a battle condition. It will exhaust itself very soon. The body will deplete energy faster. The body is on the battleground. Even if you eat food, it will be eaten and digested in the way it must be on the battleground. So, chest breathing is the wrong way of breathing unless you are running or you are genuinely in a dangerous situation. When dogs are after you, then you really need to have a fight and flight system on. At that time, breathing from the chest is required. But the rest of the time, you should not be shallow breathing from the chest.

The proper way of breathing is abdominally. Your abdomen should go in and out, in and out while you are breathing. Now, it's not that the air goes from the lungs all the way to your abdomen. It doesn't work that way. It's just that when you push the abdomen in and out, the internal organs will expand, especially the lungs, and get more space to expand.

And the more the lungs can expand, the more oxygen they can take in. So, you need to breathe from the abdomen. That's the proper way of breathing. But a lot of you people, those who are doing sitting jobs or are very stressed or if you are struggling with your physical condition, health or anything like that, then the musculature that is needed for deep breathing is missing. Missing means you have distorted your own way of breathing.

For example, posture gets distorted, right? If you keep on slouching, after some time, your upper body will bend and crouch, even when you do not need it to. Every time, your normal posture will be as if you're still sitting in a slouched way. So, this is how you distort your way of breathing, and you cannot deep breathe. So, you must practice conscious deep breathing. You can do a few simple exercises.

The first thing is to start becoming aware of that shallow breathing for the next ten days, all day long, as many times as possible, day and night. Whenever you can think of it, just pay attention to your own breathing, and see if it is shallow breathing. Don't fix it. No need to fix it for seven days, ten days, don't fix it. And if you think you are having a hard time remembering how you are breathing or paying attention to your breath, just write with the marker on your head, on your hand. Or you can write it on the notes here and there and everywhere or add an alarm to your mobile.

Wherever you are working or in your house or everywhere, pay attention to breathing; focus on breathing. I used to tell people to write FOB (Focus on Breath) on their hand with a permanent marker or a pen so they could just look at it. Or many people have Fitbit watches, or they have an alarm system on their laptops or mobile phones or iPads.

So, for seven to ten days, just go on bringing your awareness to your breath and breathing.

The second thing, for seven to ten days, just go on deep breathing. Every time you realize that you are shallow breathing, start deep breathing; do not make an excuse like "oh, I was busy"; "I was doing this, or I was doing that." What kind of work can you do which doesn't require breathing, or can you even survive without breathing? You cannot. So, you should not use excuses like "oh, I'm writing an email; how can I focus on deep breathing?" Don't focus on deep breathing; just deep breathe while writing an email. Just keep on deep breathing while working on your computer, doing any office work, or walking here and there.

If there are no dogs after you, or if there is no lion after you, there's no emergency, then you must be deep breathing. These are two important small exercises to do to fix the breathing pattern and breathing musculature.

The third practice is to do full breathing, breathing from your chest as well as your abdomen. That is also called complete breathing, and that is the ideal way to breath. You should be breathing like that most of the time. Practice it consciously for 30 days.

So, in a nutshell, you must spend at least 30 to 40 days learning to breathe properly and fix your breathing before you start any kind of yogic practice, yoga or meditation camp or any kind of program or you go to any guru; before even learning any of the 72 types of Pranayamas, you need to learn how to breathe.

You cannot do Pranayama if you do not know deep breathing and full breathing. Pranayamas are set breathing patterns that occur in a normal human being in different situations. Every 90 minutes, your breath automatically moves from the left nostril to the right, and so on. But because it is not shifting from left to right and right to left automatically, then you must be taught an anulom-vilom Pranayama to fix it. But before even you start any simple Pranayama, you need to first take a deep breath.

Learn how to breathe and function properly. Now, those who have problems with their musculature, there was a scientist who created a means of fixing that, and she did all the research for those people whose musculature of breathing gets distorted, and they cannot breathe.

So, there are scientific techniques and treatments to learn to breathe properly. Even when you learn to ride a bike, work out in a gym, study singing or playing a musical instrument, or join a yoga meditation camp, anything that you do in your life, if you want to succeed, then you need to learn proper breathing.

You cannot grow six-pack abs without learning breathing techniques properly. You cannot lose weight if you do not know how to breathe.

So, everything is connected to breathing. There's a preparatory period which is like 30 to 40 days before you go for such things.

You do that preparation first and then go and start your activities, meditation, and spiritual practices. And you will see there is a tremendous amount of difference between how you did everything with shallow breathing and then later when you do it with proper deep breathing.

The outcome is much better when you deep breathe. Try to test it yourself. When you focus your attention on how you are breathing, it develops awareness of the breath.

If you have a hard time putting your awareness or focus on your breath or if it prevents you from working, then fine . . . just deep breathe. Don't put focus or attention there. For now, just learn to breathe properly.

INCREASE SATTVA

There are three basic gunas or material items that this entire world and those in it are made up of, including you. Sattva, Rajas, and Tamas are three basic particles of creation. In short, you can understand that Sattva is the purest thing in you. It's light; it's the purest aspect of you. Then Rajas is the active aspect of you, the highly unstable and super active aspect of you, and then Tamas is the stable aspect of you, the gravity in you.

If we are talking about increasing Sattva, don't think that Tamas is bad just because it's about gravity or that you are trying to fly high somewhere, so it's a bad thing. No, you cannot sit if there is zero mass in you. You cannot walk with balance in a particular direction if there is no Tamas in you. You cannot sleep at night if there is no Tamas in you. So don't think that these gunas are good or bad. It's not about that. It's just that we must bring them to equilibrium. We must bring them to a balance so that there shouldn't be a lot of one type of Guna. For example, an imbalance of Rajas means a lot of activity, not just physical but even mental. That means you'll not have a sound sleep, or you may suffer from some form of insomnia, or you may be trying to focus on something, and your mind is running everywhere, and you will feel a lack of energy, restlessness, anxiety, may get panic attacks. Hence, understand that we have to balance these three gunas to be able to live healthy, live consciously, and be able to do one-pointed focus (Dharana) and Meditation (Dhyana) or other spiritual practices.

How to balance? The answer to this question depends upon how much imbalance is there. How much disturbance and pollution is there as a result of different sheaths (Koshas) of your gross body? Are you physically sound, without any diseases? Do you have an over-functional mind? Then the most important thing is to actually do pranayama so that it can calm down your mind. But if you were in public places, such as your office or the hospital or you travelled on public transport here and there, you absorb a lot of energy and your energy body has become very disturbed. That is causing your mind to go into thousand places and run at the speed of 10,000 thoughts per second or so. If that is the case, the best thing to do is take a shower. In other words, is your gross existence under attack temporarily, or have you induced permanent disturbance? Taking a shower increases Sattva in you; doing pranayama increases Sattva in you. It brings down Rajas, and it brings down Tamas. Listening to devotional songs or any guru's lecture or anything that creates a spark of wisdom in you that ignites your intellect and expands your consciousness increases Sattva in you. So that's why we say people should read books and scriptures to inspire themselves.

They can read the biographies of other Yogis and other people who have successfully walked their spiritual journey. You can read about them or can listen to their lectures, or you can go to them personally. Going to the Guru is another way to increase your Sattva, but only when you have devotion within and surrender (Samarpan). You may be in front of the Guru, yet you may be full of Tamas and full of Rajas. Your mind may be everywhere else except being with the Guru in that moment. If the balance between Sattva, Rajas and Tamas is disturbed, then you will not be where you are. That is why it is very important. So, you stay in your body and stay where your body is and not go on sightseeing where your body is not.

The balance of Sattva, Rajas and Tamas must be maintained by all seekers, by all Yogis, and Sattva must be increased by whatever practices you can do. Some of them are like taking a shower, doing pranayama, singing, or chanting mantras and devotional songs, doing all your yogic practices, eating sattvic food, raw green fruits and vegetables, green leafy vegetables, eating herbs and all these things. They all increase Sattva.

Living with Yama and Niyama and doing Pratyahara is the most efficient spiritual practice to increase the Sattva in a guaranteed manner. Integrity and authenticity are two of the most important outcomes of increasing Sattva in you.

I remember that, for nearly two years, when I was walking my spiritual journey, I almost became herbivorous. I was eating raw food, a lot of things, just raw herbs and plants. It naturally happens to you. But when Sattva starts rising, you cannot eat just anything and everything. You cannot eat everybody's cooking; most especially, you cannot eat any commercially cooked food or eat in restaurants. So, keep on doing things that increase Sattva in you.

Anybody who has prepared the food or cooked the food with good emotions or emotions of bhakti or when devotion is the emotion, that goes into the food, and that's when food becomes Sattvik (contains more Sattva). If you are killing somebody in your head and if you are cooking at that time, then you are making the food poisonous; you are killing its vital energy. At such times that you are not happy and balanced, you should not cook at all. We cook for our children as well. I still cook for children in the house and for my family and cook with mantras and chantings and devotions or at least love for family members; at least that much should be there while cooking. So that's when the food becomes Sattvik. Sattvik food does not just mean that you eat raw green vegetables and eat vegetarian sattvik food. I may give you a piece of cilantro while thinking about killing somebody in my head, and then the pranic energy of that vegetable or that fruit or that herb will go down. It will become Tamsik (contain more Tamas); it will become poison, and it will harm you. So, it's not just the type of food. It is also about cooking. It is also a matter of how you are occupying it or how you are acquiring that food, from where you are doing and then how you are consuming it, who has cooked it and who has prepared it.

Anybody who wants to go to pluck cilantro or when you are eating cilantro, you can just say thank you. Be in gratitude that you are eating that. So, all these things increase Sattva in you.

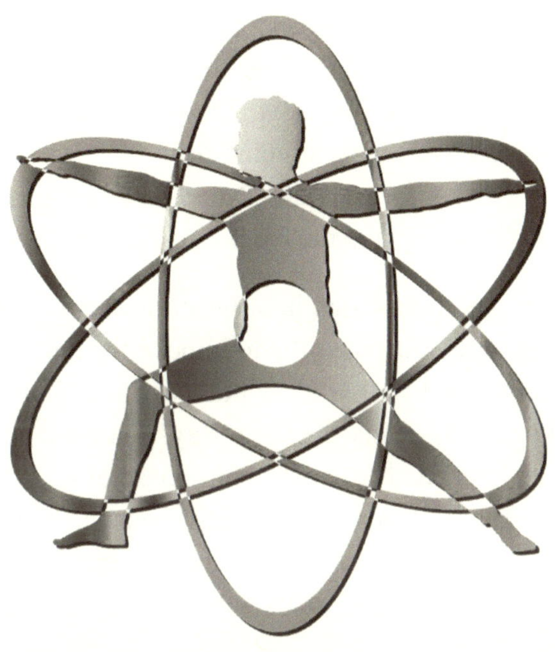

EXPAND CONSCIOUSNESS

The Hindi or Sanskrit word for consciousness is Chetna or Chaitanya. So, how to increase or expand or evolve your consciousness? See, consciousness is in everyone who is conscious or not so conscious or even unconscious. Plants have it, too, to a lesser degree than human beings. Consciousness is present in all human beings in full quantity. It's not that we have created more, or we can create more. It's just that we must evolve it, expand it, and stop the leakage.

We have to work with that which blocks it, stops it, or makes it leak away. It's like, for example, a river flowing down from a mountain. Now, if you want to ask how I take this river as far as possible or maintain or expand its flow, well, remove all the blockages, remove all the stones that are stopping it, and fill up all holes that may reduce the flow. The river that flows from the top of a mountain, a river that is coming from the glacier, when blocked by higher terrain, forms a lake. Now, how do I increase the size of this lake? Well, remove the blockages that you have built.

So, this is exactly like that light which is everywhere. Do we need to work directly with the light to remove the darkness or to expand the light? No, we must work with that which blocks it to remove the darkness. In exactly the same way, you must remove the blockages to expand or evolve your consciousness. Now, what are those blockages? Your Chitta Vrittis, your mental, emotional and behavioural patterns. You must remove them. You start with removing your likes and dislikes.

First, you must remove the duality at the smallest, lowest level, which is the likes and dislikes in your daily life. Then move on to something even much stronger and harder in you. Your anger blocks it; your hatred towards anyone blocks your consciousness. In other words, what we are saying is when you are angry, you have lost your consciousness. You are not being conscious when you are in anger or when you are in guilt, or when you are in your grief. Remove these blockages. We are not saying we don't get angry. How can you control that if you are an angry person or if you have lost somebody in your life and you are sad about it, or you are grieving about it and there is no switch to just stop things just like that? You must understand them; you have to do a little introspection, and you have to understand them. It's an acceptance that is required.

You are a human being; you are born with a human body. So, you are born with Chitta Vrittis, greed, fear, anger, raga or attachments and dwesha or aversion towards people, places and things. There is no switch to turn them off, but you can stop reacting to these states. When you are angry, yes, you have the right to be angry. You might be angry about something, but stop your reaction, just for a few minutes, and breathe in those moments. Deep breathe, do Bhastrika, do Kapal Bhati or do some other Pranayama when you are hit by any of your mental, emotional, or behavioural patterns when you are hit by any of your Chitta Vritti (psychological pattern). Just simply breathe; it will pass. That moment or those few minutes will pass. That is all that you must do to start with. Do not react out of those emotions or emotional turbulences. Do not react and strengthen those psychological patterns in you. Yes, you will feel pain, and this does not mean that your anger will go away, your grief will go away, or your emotional pain will go away. No, we are not trying to run away from our own design, the very essence of human nature. We are not trying to run away from that. We are just accepting it, giving it a space in our existence. Give space to happiness in your existence; you give space to joy in your existence; you give space to love in your existence, and, similarly, give space to grief and sadness for the time being in your existence.

There is another side of the coin. Another side of the coin requires acceptance as well . . . no need to run away from it. Just breathe in those moments. Do not react because if you do, that pattern is solidified in you. But instead of reacting out in those moments or doing something crazy or saying something crazy to yourself or to anybody else, it's not just the matter that out of anger or grief, you shouldn't be saying things or doing things to others; it is way more important to not say or do anything towards yourself. So do not react in those moments. Just breathe in those moments. Let those moments or few minutes pass by, and you will have the strength to fight back. You will have your strength, the place of power in you; a normal response then will come out. A normal response may be as simple as asking a question about what is there to be sad about or how long am I going to be sad about this or how long am I going to be angry about this, or why am I punishing myself? These kinds of questions will come only when you first accept that yes, you are angry, yes, you are in grief, and yes, it hurts the head. Accepting, introspecting and having the right perspective about life situations and people is how you remove your blocks. Before removing a block, you must break it into pieces. You go step-by-step. Right now, what happens is if you are angry, you will throw things, say it's something trash to others, or you will just keep on beating yourself in your head, and you will be angry at yourself. If you are grief-stricken, you will just stay feeling sad without even asking a question about why you are punishing yourself for so long. So, in those moments, whenever the emotional, mental, or behavioural pattern arises in you, just deep breathe.

Practice Pranayama in those very moments. Stop thinking for a moment. No thinking, no analysis of it. Deep breathe. It will cut that pattern like a sword, and suddenly you will have an expansion of your consciousness. You will be able to stop the wastage or leakage of your consciousness and will progress towards the evolution of your consciousness from where the question will arise in you that you start asking "why".

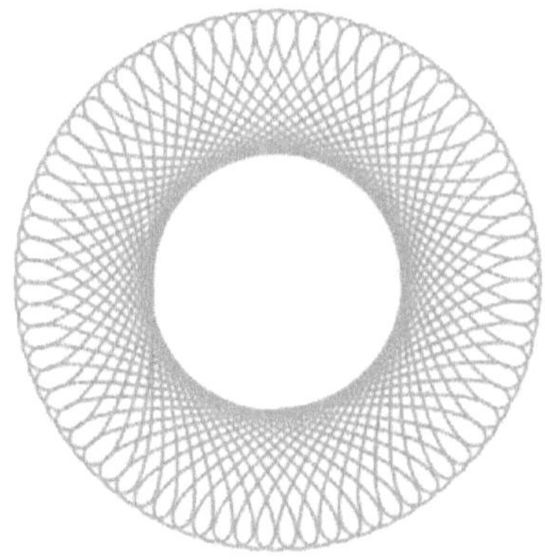

INCREASE AWARENESS

How is awareness different from Consciousness? That is the first thing to understand before you can increase or do something about your awareness. You are a Soul, Spirit, and Atma. One of the characteristics of Atma is Chetna, which means being Conscious, and one of the characteristics of Chetna or Consciousness is Awareness. Atma and Consciousness have several additional characteristics.

What does Consciousness become Aware of in the first place? The ideal state of Chetna or Consciousness is when it becomes aware of itself, and then it becomes aware of Atma (True Self, Real Self, Higher Self), who you truly are. This is an ideal state. But when you take human form, you are born with psychological patterns (Chitta-Vrittis). Then Consciousness loses its awareness of the Self, of the Atma that you are, the Real you who you are. In other words, it becomes unaware of the Self/Atma. If it is not aware of the Self/Atma, then what is it aware of? Well, it is aware of the houses you buy, the cars you purchase, the things that you do, the relationships that you have, all the things that you like, you dislike, or you hate, or you fear, or you fear losing, your desires – it becomes aware of all of that. If this is not the case, then stop being aware of all that you have and all that you are not, and place your awareness on the Real you, the Self/Atma. Can you do that? That is the moment of Enlightenment or Self-Realization or Atma-Bodha or Atma-Sakshatkara, as we call it in Hindi/Sanskrit.

For now, since you cannot do that, your awareness is scattered outwards, is scattered in this whole Samsara, in this world. The more dispassion you have within towards the Samsara (Cyclic nature of the world), the much better your focus will be on your awareness. Focused on what? Your own inner world. The less you put your mind to who is doing what or who is saying what or who is going where or why is this person doing that, in this place or in that place, in this relationship and that relationship and this breakup and that marriage and that divorce, new house, new stuff, new experiences, the less your life becomes about anything outside of you and generally becomes more about what is within.

Yoga and Pranayama techniques are taught to take this control of your own Consciousness and use it inwards.

But it's one thing like hiding sweets from a person with a sweet tooth and controlling him externally, and it's a totally different thing that that person someday has dispassion towards sweets and stops indulging themself. Then even though such a person may be standing in front of the ice cream shop, he'll not have the temptation to go inside. There may be a variety of sweets or chocolate cake and this and that in front of that person, but still, he may not have the desire to pick up a piece and put it in his mouth. So, you see, to increase awareness, we must first integrate it, meaning that the way it is aimed at different places, people, or things outside of you must stop; it has to come back within, all of it. It must be focused on your inner world. What are you thinking or why are you thinking or how your emotions changing when you are angry, yes, I am angry or when you are grief-stricken, yes I am in grief right now, yes, I want to be lonely right now? So instead of this person or that person or this place or that place or this thing or that thing, when life becomes only about you, your awareness turns within. Then you are the least bothered about what the heck is happening around you.

So, in order to increase your awareness, first at least become aware of the fact that your awareness is running outside, running wild outside towards how many things or how many people or how many events or how many memories are in your head about the past events. Start seeing that. You cannot do this just by wishing for it. There's no way. Your awareness will be controlled by the external world unless you have done some yogic sadhana or some Tapasya in some lifetime. Just by wishing, just by intention, it is not going to happen. Then how is it going to work? Well, start doing pranayams. Pranayama is a very powerful way to increase your awareness.

At first, it will become aware of all that is outside of you, then it will become aware of all that is inside you, and when everything is known, and no dark nook and corner remains anywhere, then it becomes aware of the Self, the Real You. That is when we call it Pure Consciousness. Then it becomes aware of the Atma who you are. Then it is, laser-like, pointed on to the Atma, the Real Self. Scattered light cannot cut anything, but when that light is concentrated enough and is focused on one thing, it becomes a laser beam.

It can cut through. Until the time it is scattered, it's light like a lightbulb in our house. It's not going to cut through our bodies or our mind or anything else. So, you must make it strong. You must concentrate on it. How? By pulling it from everything that it runs towards, other than You. So do Pranayamas and learn to do some yoga, and that way, your awareness will start becoming like a laser beam.

INCREASE PRANIC SHAKTI

Pranic Shakti or Pranic Energy is the Vital Force of Life within you. What depletes it in the first place? A lot of Pranic energy is consumed by working out, living life, just whatever you are doing. Whatever you do drains your Pranic energy. But that's hardly 1%, or 5% max, through living life by doing mundane things, cooking food, doing groceries, paying your bills, running here and there, doing chores, driving, taking a shower, and brushing your teeth. All that is less of a cause for depleting the Pranic energy. Indulging in sexual intercourse consumes Pranic power. The ovum is not released in women during intercourse, so their Pranic energy is not depleted horribly by having sex unless that man has low energy, low pranic shakti himself or has multiple sex partners.

In men, Pranic energy is depleted by having sex because the seed of life, the sperm, is released and has gone out of the body. Now he will need more Pranic power to produce it again. In women, Pranic energy is depleted during their menstrual cycle. But women cannot escape that; it has to happen; it's the nature of life. It's a normal thing to happen that the ovum, if it is not being used to create a child in them, will be released from the body, and in removing it, Pranic energy is lost. And also, during ovulation, the body is consuming a very large amount of Pranic energy. These are a few ways that deplete Pranic energy. Now, to save your Pranic energy, don't try to stop your periods. Don't try to mess or play with your menstrual cycle. Let it happen naturally.

Touching many people, those who are so damn crazy or have so many complexes and solidified mental, emotional, and behavioural patterns, makes you lose your Pranic energy. Whether you are a man or a woman, having sex with people or those who have multiple partners makes you quickly lose your Pranic power.

Whether you are:
- A man or a woman.
- Being in the company of crazy people.
- Complaining people.
- Listening to someone's rant all the time makes you deplete your Pranic energy.

You are drained of your Pranic energy in the company of negative social people. When someone around you is angry all the time, throwing fits and tantrums all the time, it depletes your panic energy. Most of the time, they are the family members living in the house, so there's no way for you to run away from them. But, if it's a possibility, I would say go ahead. Your first duty is towards your Self/Atma, your sanity, and keeping yourself sane. If you are not helping yourself, you can never help anybody else. So, figure out ways to stay away from them and give yourself a time-out from those who deplete your Pranic energy. These are all the external causes that consume your Pranic energy.
One major internal cause that depletes your Pranic energy is when you are in a negative state of mind; in your head, you are beating somebody or yourself, or you are cursing somebody, or you are angry about something for a long time in your head, or you are just sad, or you are in grief, or you are in some depression – all this

depletes your Pranic energy. Any negative emotion arising within you will drain your Pranic energy. An overly functional mind depletes your Pranic fuel the most. By an overactive mind, I mean all the time, some chatter is happening in your head. You will realize one thing, those who have a constant conversation in their mind or those who are constantly thinking about this and that or fears, insecurities, losing this, losing that or what if this happens or what if that happens or what if this person says that or what if that person feels this way, this is how I will defend myself, I will say this. Then I will say that, or if this person does this, then I will do this, or if this happens, then I will do some future planning, past planning, something going on in your head all the time. That is what depletes 80% of your Pranic energy. Nothing else saps such huge amount.

So, what do you need to do to increase it? First, stop up that damn hole. If you want to have some money in your pocket, your pocket cannot have a cavity. So first, eliminate all those holes, externally as well as internally. Externally, you can stop by running away or dodging people or staying away from negative people or the kind of people who are always saying negative things about themselves or other people or all the time, having some sad story, one or the other. Their morning starts with complaining about everything. Stay away from those kinds of people. And when it comes to sex, you can minimize that. Or you can choose the right partner or decide not to have it at all or not with this person or that person. You can take care of that part as well. What about mind chatter, which depletes the 80%? That is also the reason for you to age faster. People with anxiety, a worrying mind, worrying about everything and anything as if they are running the world, that is what they think.

So, what to do about that? External things can be stopped. How to control the internal problems? For those, you must do Pranayam. That is the only thing. Pranayamas are a way to put a kind of restraint on your mind. The horses of mind need to be controlled. How to do it? Sit and do 30 minutes of pranayams every day. Do 30 minutes three times a day or 30 minutes twice a day. Slowly, over the period, say, two or three months down the line, you will see a drastic change in yourself. You will have fewer anxiety attacks, fewer panic attacks, less fearfulness, and fewer problems. And then some of you will have already reached a level where you have controlled the external factors. They are not depleting your Pranic energy. You have commanded your mental chatter and now, from time to time, solidified Chitta vrittis; your mental, emotional, and behavioural patterns will knock you off of your Pranic energy completely. Then you will focus on your mental, emotional, and behavioural patterns, and you'll start cracking them, breaking them down one by one by understanding them, by doing an introspection, by talking to your yoga teacher, by talking to your spiritual teacher, your guru and understanding them in the proper perspective. That way, your Pranic energy will reach the level of the Cosmos. There is only one Prana. There is only one Pranic Shakti. And you will be able to get to that level where it never ends. Nothing impacts you. Nothing takes away your Pranic energy. You can reach that level. Until then, keep on increasing it. Do the Pranayam thrice a day, 30 minutes or 45 minutes or an hour. It will be increased to the extent that nothing matters; nothing outside and nothing inside matters.

CELIBACY

How vital is celibacy when it comes to walking your spiritual journey? We need to look at this question from different perspectives. For males, we must look at it differently because their bodies are diverse. For females, we must look at it in another way. We have different rules, regulations, paths, and different issues regarding a female body. One essential thing to understand is that it's not suppression. You do not have to suppress your bodily needs. That is one thing. But it doesn't mean you go on wasting your energy here and there, whether you are male or female. Don't go on wasting your power because your bone marrow creates your blood. And it takes a lot of Pran Shakti (Life's Vital Force) to make blood.

An even more vital life force, energy is needed to create the seed of life in you, which you call sperm. Hence, we usually ask males to follow celibacy strictly because the very act of discharging semen will seriously deplete their vital life force. In males, the secretion of semen or ejaculation of semen forces their entire existence to shut down all other life processes, pull themselves from all the different body functions and make themselves busy with producing that which is lost. The more you ejaculate, the more you lose your semen, and the more body or your life energy must work to make it again. That is why we say that males should follow celibacy if they want to raise their Kundalini and keep up with their spiritual practices. But if it goes all the way into your head in the name of spirituality, if you go on suppressing your sexual needs, then every time you are just thinking about it and burying it. Don't do that.

It's the same thing with fasting. If you are fasting, but mentally, you go on thinking about food and your hunger, then it's useless. And that's not fasting because the control is not physical. It's a renunciation, very intense renunciation. When it comes from within you, you are naturally following Brahmacharya. Now, celibacy is just one aspect of Brahmacharya. Brahmacharya doesn't mean just being celebrated. That is how a male's body works.

So, males should be celibate and should follow celibacy. Now, we need to look at another perspective: if they are a member of a family, have a wife or a husband, then sex should be exercised in moderation. Twice a month or once a month is fine; that's moderate for some people. Three times a month should be alright. So, you have to figure out your frequency because you will slowly start understanding what happens to you when you ejaculate, and your semen is gone. What exactly your body does? How does your energy become? You will start noticing those subtle things.

So, you have to come to define your baseline. What is your definition of moderation? You have to explain it by yourself. What is moderation for you? What is moderation for one person may not be the same for another. Now those who have taken sannyasa and are official sanyasis from the world do not have a family. So for them, if they can be celibate, that's the best thing. That's the best thing because their life energy is not being used. So now you can use life energy to awaken each Chakra and, ultimately, when all chakras are awakened, Kundalini will awaken. Kundalini will not obstruct the path, and Kundalini immediately shoots up. So that is about men.

With the female body, it's a different thing. Why? With the female body, it's dealing with it psychologically. Whenever females indulge in sexual acts, they are not releasing the ova in their bodies. Their body and life force are never involved in the creation of the ovum as women are born with a set number of ova. Their discharge does not consist of the seed of life so that they can have sex, and it won't impact them or bring their energy down, or it won't use up their Pranic energy (Life's vital force). So, for women, being celibate from the point of view of Pranic Shakti does not matter much. But women menstruate every month and when they are ovulating, their Pranic energy is depleted.

So, women cannot escape this cycle, and it's very much necessary for their existence and the body they carry. There is no escape from that. We are bound by nature so that it will happen. And because of menstruation, all toxins from the body are released, and the body attains a healthy balance, which is lost for a variety of reasons or simply due to living a stressful life.

Men do not have any natural detoxification process and or way to balance their physical/gross existence. Hence, men need to have control. If they do not discharge and can hold and become celibate, they definitely can have a better chance of holding their own Pranic Shakti and not wasting it. Whether you are male or a female, one essential thing to understand is that it's not just a matter of Pranic Shakti when it comes to celibacy; it is also a matter of the fact that you do not want to mix your energy with that of somebody else because your sadhana or your spiritual practices purify your energy. It makes your mind become calm and focused. You will have less disturbance throughout the day.

When you become intimate with somebody, you lose energy because no matter what you do, whenever two people are intimate, one will absorb the other's energy. Usually, it's the purity in one person or the purity of the energy that will absorb the unclean thing. Then you may think that you can take a shower and be fine and go back to your spiritual practices and your Tapasya. No, it does not work that way. For at least seven to ten days, the impact of the other person's energy will not be gone from your energy body, or that energy will still be hanging on to your energy body, to your etheric body. So that is an even more important reason to become a celibate and to follow Brahmacharya and not just be a celibate.

We usually do Pranam or Namaste to people we meet. It would be best if you did not go on shaking hands and hugging people until you have the balance in your energy body, etheric body, until you can safeguard your energy and are mature enough that no matter who you touch or are intimate with, your body is powerful enough and strong enough to handle any disturbances. It would be best if you were celibate because you don't want to absorb other people's thoughts and psychological patterns (Chitta-Vrittis) and whatever goes on in their minds and emotions.

Another essential thing to remember for both males and females is that you should not indulge with a partner with multiple partners. If you do, then there is no way you will be able to walk your spiritual journey and progress spiritually. Every time you do so, your energy will start coming down. And not just that, you will have body pains. You will be sick with unexplainable kinds of pains in your head; you will have shoulder pains, you will have back pain, and your entire body will start aching. That's what happens when you touch someone who has multiple partners or partners other than you. So don't do that. These are why we ask spiritual seekers not to be intimate with others. Exercise caution, exercise moderation. And if you are female, don't worry so much about sex from the point of view that it will bring your Pranic Shakti down and will not help you raise your Kundalini. But if you can do that, it's helpful for your spiritual practices for other reasons. Female Brahmacharya is different from male Brahmcharya. Female celibacy is more about not touching others' bodies due to higher sensitivity and energy/Shakti. For men, private body parts are energy absorbers, energy sponges. But for females, their entire body works like a big energy sponge, especially when pursuing the spiritual journey. Females should not stay longer even in the city surroundings, noise and people and corporates where many psychological patterns are at play. If you can skip that and somehow go away for some time, do that. Go to the mountains, go to natural places, and relax. Be in nature as much as possible. Because people, surroundings will impurify your energy. The city people, the city life, the food, the chaos all around you and the people with lots of thoughts and junk in their heads will impurify your energy.

Nature, their surroundings, the mountains, lakes and valleys – all that purifies your energy. It just uplifts your energy. So be in nature as much as possible, whether you are a man or a woman.

If you are serious about your spiritual journey, those with a male body, then be a celibate or go for moderation. If you are a female with a family, don't worry so much about having sex because you don't release the ovum. But yes, when you have your menstrual cycle, avoid touching anybody at that time . . . not even hugging or anything, just no physical touch at all. Females stand a perfect chance of absorbing anything negative or impure during ovulation and menstruation. Hence, females have different rules and parameters to follow.

And whether you are male or female, please do not touch anybody with a partner other than you; it makes your entire existence chaotic and disturbed. You will progress quickly through your spiritual practices if you keep all this in mind. Understand that these restrictions are not for forever. Once you're done with your spiritual journey and you, as life has evolved, your energy, your etheric body, has grown and expanded, this won't impact or matter so much. But then you don't want to do it. That's a different story because your physical boundary does not limit you. Anything involving your gross physical existence seems to feel less intense and less valuable to you. There's no intensity in that which is gross compared to the Parmananda (Divine Bliss). When you are becoming more subtle, what you get from Samadhi will never be equivalent to all these small things like touching other people or intimately touching somebody or going for all these things. It doesn't hold any significance afterwards.

MINIMIZE KARMA

How to minimize Karma? For that, the most important key factor is to be mindful, to increase your awareness so that you can stop and catch yourself when it is happening in your mind. And further actions based on your psychological patterns (Chitta Vrittis) can be prevented. For example, in your mind, you want to slap somebody. Still, when you are about to strike them, the moment when the desire happens or the Karma happens, or the intention happens that I should slap somebody and between physically hitting somebody, guiding your hand to crash land on someone's cheek, there is a time lag. There is a time lag between thought and action. If you are conscious, then you can stop action. You must become aware and mindful of your ideas to avoid having such an intention. Karma has to be stopped on three levels because it has three elements. It is done through speech. You may not physically slap someone, but your words may be enough for them to experience so much pain that it feels like you have beaten them badly. So, words are equally powerful and you may be doing Karma through your speech. So, the intention of slapping someone, saying that I am about to beat you, or I will hit you and then actually punching someone – three things are there; Intention, Thought, Speech or Action. Karma has to be stopped at all three levels, and that can only happen if you increase your awareness and expand your consciousness. How do you raise your awareness? How can you always be more mindful? By practicing yama, niyama, asana, pranayama, pratyahara, dharana and dhyana. Those who have already landed in lower Samadhi will not ask this question. The more you stay within your spiritual practices, the lesser the chance to interact with other people or the world; that way, Karma goes down. Who has time for all the nonsense in the world? Don't interact with people; keep doing your spiritual practices and learning every day. If you look at the kind of pressures that are there these days for earning money and sustaining life, just that much is enough to occupy a lot of your time. When do you have time to create more Karma? You do your job, take a shower, clean your house, cook food, buy groceries, and get your maintenance done for this thing or that thing or pay your bills and do all that stuff, and whatever time is remaining, you are doing your spiritual practices, and you are relaxing in between. You don't have much time left to create Karma. Still, some people find time to make a lot of Karma because no matter where they are, whether working in the office or factory, they'll have sinister intentions for others or themselves. No matter what their body is busy with, their mind is more active in strengthening the deep-dark psychological patterns (Chitta-Vrittis). When you are physically busy, Karma mostly happens through your mind, via your intentions. You may always beat someone or kill someone in your head. It would help if you became aware and stopped doing that. It would be best if you minimized it to a level that limited the overall impact of Karma on yourself.

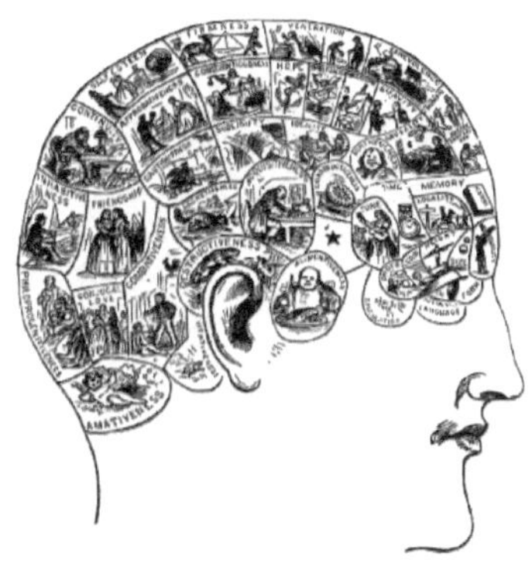

SCIENCE OF KNOWLEDGE and KNOWING

How do you know all that you know? Did you ever ask that question to yourself? Were your beliefs and convictions formed because of your direct experiences? Or were they instilled by society? Or do they have no solid basis or foundation?

To inquire within, you need to know the science of knowing or the science of knowledge. How do you know or attain knowledge of anything in this world, in life?

There are only three ways to know anything, everything –
　　1.　Direct Experience (Hindi/Sanskrit – Pratyaksh)
　　2.　Inference
　　3.　Testimony (verbal, written, etc.)
These are the three ways of knowing through which anything and everything is known to humans. Now, let's get into the detail of each one.

Direct Experience (Hindi/Sanskrit - Pratyaksha)

You have five senses of perception: vision, hearing, taste, touch and smell. These senses work through your physical organs: eyes, ears, tongue, skin and nose, respectively. You perceive and experience life using these sense organs, and you know about the physical world around you through them as well. Different people may have a diverse range of vision and/or hearing and hence the perception or experience of the same thing may vary among them. Other people may have a different body or environmental conditions to impact their senses and reduce their ability to perceive or know.

For example, food may taste bitter when one is on specific medication or is sick. Another example, a rope may be mistaken for a snake if it is dark. Even when someone's senses are working perfectly, they have no problems in their body and environmental conditions also are right, the range of senses is limited. For example, you cannot see the planet Pluto with your eyes without the help of a telescope. Even if you can see it through a scientific telescope, you may not know many things like temperature, the climate of the planet, its cycles of weather, or the length of day and night compared to earth. Even though you see the sun daily, you cannot fathom its surface temperature or closest orbit. So, environmental conditions, body conditions and the range of the five senses may cause an error of perception.

Upon realizing that, in the modern era, human senses might not be a foolproof way of gathering knowledge, the need for scientific equipment became the mother of invention and the basis for most modern technology.

Now, even when all your senses are working in a hundred per cent ideal condition, is everything a subject of your senses? Can anything and everything be known through those five senses? For example, can you see, hear, taste, touch or smell "love" or any other feeling? Yes, people may talk or act or react based on feelings of love or any other emotion, but without perceiving their talk or actions/reactions through the five senses, is there another way to know that love exists or that so and so person loves you? Sixth sense. Yes, through the sixth sense, your intuition, your intuitive body, you can know a lot that cannot be perceived through the five senses. So, anything "subtle" in nature is not a subject of the five senses. Some people are empathetic and can know the feelings or mental-emotional states of other people through intuition, or as another's state is replicated in them. You cannot correctly know love, devotion, and wisdom in others if only five senses are used. So, never say that just because you have not seen, heard, tasted, touched, or smelled something, it doesn't exist. Because the most beautiful feelings and things outside the range of the five senses exist. Love exists, and so does Pluto.

Not everything is a subject of five senses because five senses are a minimal way of perception. You cannot perceive existential reality and life through the five senses. Hence, relying solely on your limited instruments of perception is not a wise thing to do. Having an open mind and allowing your intuitive body to expand will greatly help you.

Now, only in Indian culture and civilization, we find the technology of Yogic Science, which gives us the techniques to expand Consciousness through sensory withdrawal (Pratyahara), One-Pointed Focus (Dharana) and Meditation (Dhyana) and helps people go through Samyama Samadhi (Small Samadhi where oneness is experienced with the object of Meditation). Such expansion of Consciousness results in Ritambhara Pragya, a unique, flawless state of Intellect that will allow one to know anything and everything without any doubt.

Maharishi Patanjali explains in Yoga Sutras how one can do Samyama Samadhi on the North Star, the moon, sun, galaxies, solar system, cosmos, herbs, plants, five elements, human and other being's existence, etc. to know everything about them, without dissecting or killing or destroying them. In ancient times, that's how Indian sages (Rishis) attained Ritambhara Pragya (Highly refined Intellect, Pure Consciousness) and wrote down Six Hindu Philosophies (Shad Darshan), Ayurveda, Sushruta Samhita, Charaka Samhita, Upanishads and so much information they downloaded for human welfare. They would go into Samyama Samadhi around their own Naval and knew everything about the human body without dissecting it. They did Samyama in the solar system and galaxies and knew everything about them without waiting for thousands of years for a piece of equipment to record anything. Those sages (Rishis) made their existence into the most delicate possible instruments of perception, tools of knowledge and knowing. Hence, ancient Indian culture and civilization did not need to invent scientific equipment to know Zero or Vedic Mathematics or Astrology or Science of Sound, Mantras, Yantras and Tantra and everything else.

You can also attain Ritambhara Pragya through intense spiritual practices and experience the same. It's a proven technique and has been working since ancient times. This is the highest and most efficient way of knowing. But, in this era, the so-called modern humans do not have the purity, sanctity, integrity and patience to attain Ritambhara Pragya through intense spiritual practices, hence their overreliance on sensory perception, instruments, equipment, technology and overindulgence in sensory pleasure.

In today's day and age, most people do not even understand that that which is changing can be measured through instruments, like your blood sugar or your blood pressure, solar cycles, moon phases or anything else. That which is permanent, eternal, and never changes cannot be measured through any instrument for any parameter. To know that something exists, it must not exist at some point for scientific equipment to realize it or measure it. To know that something is present, it must be absent at times. But that which is eternal, always existing, cannot be known or measured through any scientific instrument, gross instruments like the five senses. That which is infinite can only be understood by that which is eternal. Your senses exist and perceive only when you have a gross and subtle body. This means there are times when your five and sixth senses do not exist. Hence your gross, subtle existence is not eternal, but you are! The Real Self/Atma, the Paramatma/Divine-Self/Creator, are eternal; they always exist.

Hence, only Real-Self/Atma can know Paramatma/Divine-Self, the Creator.

So, no matter how good your five senses are, how sure shot your intuition is, without developing Ritambhara Pragya through intense spiritual practices, sensory withdrawal (Pratyahara), One-Pointed Focus (Dharana) and Meditation (Dhyana), you will never know the Real You (Self, Atma). Likewise, you will not know the Paramatma (Divine Self, the Creator) until you are an Atma.

To be a true Yogi is to attain Ritambhara Pragya, a high level of pure Consciousness, the highest level of Intellect allowing one to know all that is. That is when you will achieve the genuinely deepest level of direct experience and will have knowledge. This is what the Hindi/Sanskrit term "Pratyaksha" is roughly, approximately, not precisely translated as "direct experience". The English language does not have the vocabulary for subtle existence and existential reality perceivable during higher states of Consciousness.

Ritambhara Pragya is not only attained by Yogis/Rishis who were interested in learning about all that is, but also by those who were seeking Moksha/Mukti (Spiritual Liberation, Ultimate Freedom), those who were seeking Paramatma (Divine) and were seeking to know who am I (Self/Atma). In other words, Ritambhara Pragya is needed for Samyama Samadhi, all four lower levels of Samadhi (Savikalpa/Sampragyat, Savichara, Sabeeja, Sananda) and for the ultimate Samadhi (Nirvikalpa/Asampragyat/Nirbeeja) that we call as Enlightenment or Self Realisation.

Inference (Hindi/Sanskrit - Anuman)

Inference or Anuman in Hindi/Sanskrit is the second way of knowing or gathering knowledge. It is less efficient than learning through the Direct Experience or Pratyaksha. Because you stand a higher chance of inferring the correct knowledge and also because, through inference, you can know only so much in comparison to the direct experience. But still, it is a widely used method of knowing all that skipped our curiosity or desire to know during our direct experience or anything that we found less critical in any given moment.

Inference requires using fact or complete Truth as a base upon which you will infer, conclude or know. For example, suppose you see dark clouds outside and infer that it will rain. But it didn't. What went wrong? Your base. You may have noticed dark clouds, but it is not the complete Truth, as you might have failed to consider wind speed or atmospheric pressure. Hence, the knowledge that you inferred was wrong. Another example, suppose you believe, you infer, you conclude that there are no ghosts. And imagine you used the base fact, the Truth that there is no scientific evidence. Again, your conclusion is wrong because modern science is not about any subject beyond the four-dimensional perception world. Science is not absolute knowledge; it gives knowledge only in a point-in-time manner. Science itself is under development, still evolving. So, you cannot use a half-baked foundation, incomplete truth-based methodology for knowing something in the subtle world. Now, suppose, instead of scientific proof, you used the fact that you haven't seen any ghosts through direct experience. Since you are still living, you are still in the lifespan of direct experience, and it hasn't happened yet, but you stand a chance of experiencing it. Another fact may be that you may or may not have taken steps and raised your Consciousness to the level where you can perceive non-body beings like ghosts. If you keep using incomplete Truth as the basis for inference, then the knowledge you will infer will be wrong. Your conclusions and your wisdom will be wrong. You will live in illusionary knowledge or, as we call it in Hindi/Sanskrit, Bhranti Gyan.

What is being explained here is that you should keep an open mind towards existential truths and do intense spiritual practices to raise the level of Consciousness that you are on, to purify the level of Intellect that you have got to know the Truth with absoluteness. Because only absolute Truth will set you free; only that will take away your suffering. On the contrary, illusionary knowledge will further drown you in the abyss and add to your misery.

From time to time, you need to question your beliefs, your convictions, conclusions, your knowledge that is either supporting or disrupting the life that you are, that is either expanding the human potential that you could achieve or is curtailing the existential reality in you. Therefore, analysis and scrutiny of knowledge within are necessary for being a Yogi. Without this, you will not be able to decode your spiritual experiences and progress.

Testimony (Hindi/Sanskrit - Agama)

Third, the last and least efficient way of knowing, is through others' Testimony. It is less efficient in comparison to direct experience. It's not a lesser way of knowing; it's least efficient because you will know less through reading and listening to the Testimony than you would learn through direct experience.
It's one thing to experience a beautiful sunrise by yourself versus listening to someone else's description of sunrise.

The only accepted Testimony for spiritual matters, yogic sciences, and existential reality is that of ancient Indian sages (Rishis) in the form of Vedas, Upanishads, and Six Hindu Philosophies (Shad Darshan); Agama Shastras are explicitly written for this era of humanity and other ancient texts. Why? Those sages (Rishis) wrote about their direct experiences and knowledge from the state of Ritambhara Pragya. In today's age of the Internet and self-publishing, many people are sharing their experiences without developing the Ritambhara Pragya to validate their knowledge. Reading such accounts not only confuses spiritual seekers but deludes them for a long time. It's an utter waste of time and energy.

Hence, credibility establishment is necessary to accept the Testimony. The Internet is full of junk knowledge, and most spiritual seekers do not want to read profound scriptures (Shad Darshan Shastras) or ancient knowledge-based texts and accounts and end up living in their illusions.

You might have heard that ancient sages (Rishis) and Enlightened ones can directly transfer their experience and wisdom into a ready disciple who has attained Ritambhara Pragya. How? That's the beauty of Ritambhara Pragya. It has a Cosmic element; the wisdom held by it is never lost, and the container that it is, is never destroyed. But, of course, it would be best if you could read and comprehend so profoundly that you start vibing with the Ritambhara.

Pragya of the writer, the author

It is more like meditating on the words and wisdom of that book. And that is one of the sure-shot ways of gaining existential wisdom quickly. It is tremendously helpful for walking your spiritual journey, primarily if you are not relying on any human Guru. Ritambhara Pragya serves as your inner Guru. Other than these three ways of knowing, there is no other way. Hence, it would be best if you were wise enough to learn through these ways. Therefore, being a true Yogi means always being open to wisdom.

SPIRITUAL JOURNEY OF ADIGURU PRAKRITI

Introduction

The self-realised master, Adiguru Prakriti, is a reincarnated disciple of the great Kriya Yoga Guru Shri Lahiri Mahasaya. Having her Kundalini awakening in 2011, Guru Mother Adiguru Prakriti experienced enlightenment in 2015 in Jacksonville, FL. Many more months of committed spiritual practice led to full self-realisation in 2016. Born in India and now residing in Melbourne, Australia, this Yogi and spiritual teacher dedicates herself to teaching people worldwide. Guru Mother Adiguru Prakriti's journey was quite unique; holding two graduate degrees, she worked in the IT industry for 20 years before committing to the path of Self-Realisation. She also lectured at the college associated with the University of New Delhi.

She works tirelessly to support people in awakening to their Self, recognizing the dormant potential within each person and lovingly providing a plethora of wisdom and spiritual practices. Her candid talks shatter programmed belief systems and tear down the web of illusion/ignorance/Maya. As spiritual "Mother," Adiguru Prakriti helps children recognize and maintain touch with their Divine Selves. When she is not busy helping others, she loves hiking the Melbourne mountains.

Her Story

At only five years of age, Guru Mother Adiguru Prakriti knew that she was born with a significant purpose and began searching for the "unknown." Highly intuitive, she experienced an interest in lotus flowers and had bizarre dreams, many of vipers and king cobras which, when awake, she caught and played with. Not surprisingly, at age 14, Mother Kali, the goddess who destroys illusions, initiated her into renunciation. She experienced the impermanence of life in a shocking way, leading to her questioning the true nature of life, death, God, and Absolute Reality. She also came to be aware that she was living *in* the world but was not *of* it.

At that point, her path led to a traditional lifestyle of family and a career in information technology. For years, Prakriti rode the hamster wheel of successes, failures, love, loneliness – all the highs and lows most people experience.

However, in 2011, the inner urge to "know the unknown" resurfaced, and Guru Mother Adiguru Prakriti knew she had to follow it. The time had arrived to increase her meditation practice and raise her Kundalini Shakti. With no guru to guide her, she began meditating at 3:00 a.m. every morning. Inner wisdom began surfacing, including the realisation that she was the disciple of Guru Lahiri Mahasaya, the great, grand Guru of Paramahansa Yogananda.

Adiguru Prakriti's spiritual awakening quickened after practising Kundalini Kriya and dhyana for a time. Then, in December 2011, she was jolted out of her world when she caught a glimpse of Samadhi. This was the most beautiful day for her as she saw another reality that was Absolute in nature. As the Kundalini Shakti throbbed within her, the guru chakra flowered and Ritambhara Pragya stabilised in her. She started following her Inner Guru, a journey full of ups and downs. Being a scientifically minded person and with no reliance on a living guru or master to hold her hand, she questioned the highest truths about life, creation, the Universe and her own existence.

Enlightenment was experienced in 2015 after 3.5 years of arduous direct confrontation with herself. Illusions were all gone, and no more questions were left to be answered. This changed Guru Mother Adiguru Prakriti's perception completely and touched the domain of mysticism. She transcended and merged with the Divine Self (Paramatma) and experienced herself as a pure Consciousness "Being".

Wherever she looked, she saw herself. Perception expanded beyond the six senses, and she found herself One with the entire Universe, including every awakened master, every person deceased or alive. The realisation (Atma Bodh - Atma Sakshatkara) "Being One with ALL" resulted in Bliss (Paramananda) and Universal Love. Subsequently, for more than a month, she remained in Nirvikalpa Samadhi.

Eight months later, Nirvikala concluded, and it felt like she fell into Nothingness (Unmanifest/Shoonya/Shiva), went through a complete merger to the extent of becoming non-existent and had a no-self experience. She faced her own death, not of the body, but of the ego-mind. In 2016, she became Self-Realised; this brought Cosmic/Supreme Consciousness, and the "personal I/Prakriti" was destroyed forever. Now, this Supreme Consciousness/Shiva-Shakti union is in play through her body and she devotes her days to helping others achieve the same while sharing the true joy of life. A few of those who know her, after basking in the universal love, bliss, and Shakti emanating from her consciousness, lovingly gave her the name "Adiguru", which means primordial Guru/Master.

Guru Mother Adiguru Prakriti recognises that those who have gone within can genuinely experience the wonder through her and may be able to touch that Supreme Consciousness and awaken themselves. She sees herself as a "mirror" in which others can see themselves, reflections that allow them to become more conscious and awake – the whole point of being in this body.

May everyone be Awake, attain Samadhi, and be joyful and blissful through her Initiations, Retreats and Programs.

For more information, comments, and suggestions, you can email BeingShivaFoundation@yahoo.com.

www.ingramcontent.com/pod-product-compliance
Lightning Source LLC
Chambersburg PA
CBHW061358160726
47995CB00001B/367